Nebraska

By Pam Zollman

Subject Consultant
Sally Snyder
Coordinator of Children and Young Adult Library Services
Nebraska Library Commission
Lincoln, Nebraska

Reading Consultant
Cecilia Minden-Cupp, PhD
Former Director of the Language and Literacy Program
Harvard Graduate School of Education
Cambridge, Massachusetts

Children's Press®
A Division of Scholastic Inc.
New York   Toronto   London   Auckland   Sydney
Mexico City   New Delhi   Hong Kong
Danbury, Connecticut

Designer: Herman Adler
Photo Researcher: Caroline Anderson
The photo on the cover shows bluffs in Nebraska's High Plains Region.

Library of Congress Cataloging-in-Publication Data

Zollman, Pam.
  Nebraska / by Pam Zollman.
    p. cm. — (Rookie read-about geography)
  Includes index.
  ISBN 13: 978-0-516-25466-1 (lib. bdg.)   978-0-531-16814-1 (pbk.)
  ISBN 10: 0-516-25466-9 (lib. bdg.)   0-531-16814-X (pbk.)
  1. Nebraska—Juvenile literature. 2. Nebraska—Geography—Juvenile
literature. I. Title. II. Series.
  F666.3.Z65 2007
  978.2—dc22   2006004590

CHILDREN'S PRESS, and ROOKIE READ-ABOUT®, and associated
logos are trademarks and/or registered trademarks of Scholastic Library
Publishing. SCHOLASTIC and associated logos are trademarks and/or
registered trademarks of Scholastic Inc.
1 2 3 4 5 6 7 8 9 10 R 16 15 14 13 12 11 10 09 08 07

Which state is called
the Cornhusker State?
It's Nebraska!

A cornhusker is someone who removes the outer covering from ears of corn. Corn is an important crop in Nebraska.

Nebraska is in the middle of the United States. It touches six other states.

Can you find Nebraska on the map?

CANADA

WASHINGTON

OREGON

IDAHO

MONTANA

WYOMING

NORTH DAKOTA

SOUTH DAKOTA

MINNESOTA

WISCONSIN

MICHIGAN

NEW HAMPSHIRE

VERMONT

MAINE

NEW YORK

MASSACHUSETTS

RHODE ISLAND

CONNECTICUT

NEW JERSEY

NEBRASKA

IOWA

PENNSYLVANIA

NEVADA

UTAH

COLORADO

KANSAS

ILLINOIS

INDIANA

OHIO

WEST VIRGINIA

DELAWARE

MARYLAND

CALIFORNIA

MISSOURI

KENTUCKY

VIRGINIA

Washington, D.C.

ARIZONA

NEW MEXICO

OKLAHOMA

ARKANSAS

TENNESSEE

NORTH CAROLINA

TEXAS

MISSISSIPPI

ALABAMA

GEORGIA

SOUTH CAROLINA

LOUISIANA

FLORIDA

North

West   East

South

ALASKA   CANADA

MEXICO

HAWAII

5

Grasslands in Nebraska's High Plains

Nebraska has three main
land sections, or regions.
These are the Till Plains,
the Great Plains, and
the High Plains.

The Till Plains are in eastern Nebraska.

This region has rolling hills and rivers. The Platte River flows through the Till Plains.

The Platte River

A Nebraska wheat field

The Till Plains are good for farming. Farmers there grow corn, soybeans, and wheat.

The Great Plains stretch across southwestern Nebraska.

This area is rough and hilly. Many farmers here grow wheat. Others raise cattle or sheep.

Cattle graze on a farm in Nebraska.

The Loess Hills

The Loess Hills are in the Great Plains. Loess is yellow-brown dust. Wind blows loess across the area.

The High Plains are in northwestern Nebraska.

This region does not get much rain. Farmers in the High Plains must bring in water to grow their crops.

Farmers in the High Plains use special machines to water their crops.

Toadstool Park

The Badlands are part of the High Plains.

The Badlands are filled with steep hills and oddly shaped rocks. In Toadstool Park, the rocks look like mushrooms, or toadstools.

Nebraska's largest city is Omaha. Omaha is next to the Missouri River.

The second-largest city is Lincoln, the state capital.

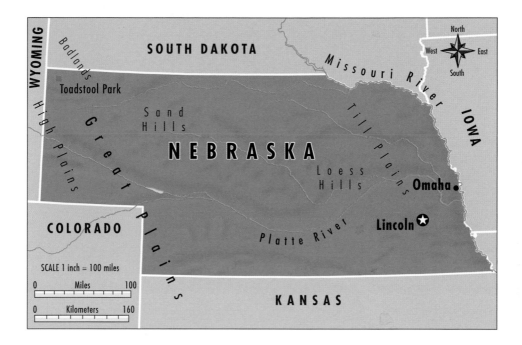

WYOMING

Badlands

SOUTH DAKOTA

North

West ✦ East

South

Missouri River

IOWA

Toadstool Park

Sand
Hills

High Plains

Great Plains

NEBRASKA

Till Plains

Loess
Hills

Omaha•

COLORADO

Lincoln ★

Platte River

SCALE 1 inch = 100 miles

0   Miles   100

0   Kilometers   160

KANSAS

A western meadowlark

Nebraska is home to birds such as falcons, loons, woodpeckers, and cranes.

The state bird is the western meadowlark.

Deer, elk, prairie dogs, and muskrats live in Nebraska, too.

Nebraska's rivers have striped bass, sunfish, bluegill, and trout. The state fish is the channel catfish.

A channel catfish

Sledders race down a Nebraska hillside.

Nebraska has hot summers. People like to play golf, ride horses, picnic, hike, fish, and swim.

Winters in Nebraska are cold. Visitors enjoy cross-country skiing, sledding, and ice-skating.

Nebraska is filled with amazing places to visit!

What would you like to do in Nebraska?

Visitors on a fishing trip in Nebraska

Words You Know

Badlands

cattle

channel catfish

Loess Hills

Platte River

sledding

western meadowlark

wheat

Index

About the Author

Pam Zollman is the award-winning author of short stories and books for kids. She is a native Texan living in the Pocono Mountains of Pennsylvania. Pam thoroughly enjoyed her visit to Nebraska. She dedicates this book to Marian Young, a friend and writer who lives in Omaha.

Photo Credits

Photographs © 2007: AP/Wide World Photos/Nati Harnik: 26, 31 top right; Chuck Haney: 17; Corbis Images: 9, 31 top left (James L. Amos), 10, 31 bottom right (Craig Aurness), 18, 30 top left (Annie Griffiths Belt); Dembinsky Photo Assoc.: 13, 30 top right (Darrell Gulin), 22, 31 bottom left (Bill Leaman); Index Stock Imagery/FogStock: 3; Joseph A. Mason/University of Wisconsin-Madison: 14, 30 bottom right; Nebraska Division of Travel and Tourism/M. Forsberg: 29; The Image Works/David R. Frazier: 6; Tom Till Photography, Inc.: cover; Visuals Unlimited/John G. Shedd Aquarium: 25, 30 bottom left.

Maps by Bob Italiano